IN AN
ECSTATIC
STATE

Many Blessings
on the Path
of Transformation.

Joseph Aldo

IN AN ECSTATIC STATE

Poems of Transformation

JOSEPH ALDO

outskirtspress
DENVER, COLORADO

In An Ecstatic State
Poems of Transformation

Outskirts Press, Inc.
http://www.outskirtspress.com

ISBN: 978-1-4787-4934-9

Outskirts Press and the "OP" logo are trademarks belonging to Outskirts Press, Inc.

PRINTED IN THE UNITED STATES OF AMERICA

"Your heart and my heart
are very, very old friends."
— Hafiz

CONTENTS

IN AN ECSTATIC STATE

A JOURNEY OF TRANSFORMATION

INTRODUCTION

In An Ecstatic State is my offering to those who are interested in exploring a reality that is beyond what this manifest world has to offer, for those who wish to find a deeper connection to their Self via the process of personal transformation.

Poetry is what got me through the many "dark night of the soul" experiences, a vehicle through which I could heal the inner wounds while establishing a way to connect and commune with God. Such a claim may sound grandiose. However, for me, such communications are simple and natural. It is my desire to make this way of communing with the source of all that is as common as speaking with our best friend. For, indeed, God *is* our best friend, no matter what name or attribute we wish to give this presence.

Many themes run throughout this poetry. Two of them are love and death, neither of which can be fully experienced without the presence of the other, for each opens the doorway for the other to be realized, to be actualized. Love is the force that draws us to the edge of the cliff, compelling us to seek something more than the known life we are living. And death . . . death pushes us off the cliff, urging us to shed the limited mind – and all of its restrictive, conditional beliefs – allowing us to be reborn into the Light, the Truth, the awakened Self. For me, this relationship between love and death is the most significant – as significant as lover and Beloved – as it initiates the journey that leads toward the ultimate relationship: the union between Self and God.

If love and death are doorways, "suffering" is the path that leads to them. I've placed suffering in quotations because what we have been conditioned to believe of suffering is but one interpretation of the experience. If we watch an expectant mother in labor, we may think she is in significant pain and consequently suffering. However, another mother who has gone through the birthing process may interpret this situation in a very different way. She may perceive this suffering as ecstasy, for what is to come from these "painful" sensations is a great gift of unequaled proportion worthy of all effort.

The limited concepts of pain and suffering have led us to fear these experiences at all cost, doing whatever possible to avoid entering these "uncomfortable" moments. Certainly, pain and suffering are not experiences that I look forward to or seek to encounter. However, I have learned that when I consciously enter into these states, I can uproot the cause of suffering, which in the moment appears painful. But in reality, like the unborn moving through the birth canal – from the known to the unknown – suffering is a journey that leads to the death of the limited self and (re)birth of the authentic, True Self.

Since the unaware, controlling mind fears the unknown, it interprets the sensations of suffering as something negative, doing whatever it can to stop these feelings from arising. We can spend our whole life avoiding the source of our suffering, thinking that we are living the life that we were born to live. However, one day we may wake up only to realize that we are living a life only partially lived, designed and directed by some external ideal. There is a way to ensure that we are living an authentic life: To die a conscious death, or as the sages of the East have taught: To die before we die.

To die before we die is the answer to the question: Who am I? For each time we delve into the mind's limited perceptions, the eternal witness within responds: "Not that. I am not that which I had thought or believed myself to be, for I am much greater than any of that which I could imagine or has imagined me to be." At some point within this inquiry, the mind begins to let go, as the witness realizes that this mental chatter we have called our Self is nothing more than a parrot spewing nonsense. More and more, the mind surrenders these false notions of Self as it awakens to the voice within, the voice of Truth or what I call, "The Wisdom of the Heart." The mind then becomes an ally on the journey back to wholeness – back to soulfulness – as it shakes off the stupor of unconsciousness.

The labyrinth of illusion is a tricky maze to maneuver, for each conscious awakening shocks the soul like a newborn slapped into this world. "What life have I been living?" "What reality has been living me?" These realizations are challenging moments to the limited personality, for when the veils of Maya lift, the eyes that now see so clearly fill with tears of a life half-lived. But these moments pass as the new vision integrates, until the next death and subsequent awakening.

Eventually, this process becomes life itself, to the point where each moment is a welcome death to the previous moment, where all attachments are released as all of life is embraced. This is, ultimately, the life that is fully lived – a moment to moment existence, judging nothing, accepting everything – for all exists in the heart of God, and nothing is separate from the Creator. These are simply words to those who have not "died a conscious death." But for those who have gone through the inner transformations – likened to the caterpillar awakening to its true essence, the butterfly – they understand with their whole being that unless this death is endured, life cannot be truly lived.

If the door of transformation is unopened, a significant part of us remains unaware, asleep in the shadows. From this perspective, we are not living a conscious life. Instead, life is living us – the conditioned and imposed ideas of life. This "life" is like a hypnotic spell, a disconnected reality filled with distracting events. And the allure of the material world – with its ever changing array of seductive promises of satisfaction – then becomes the guiding force navigating our journey, manipulating our delicate sensibilities and usurping our spiritual faculties with its self-serving agenda. This is the cost of a distracted life, where unconsciousness takes precedence in exchange for our spiritual quest.

I know, all too well, the power of Maya and the dream she weaves in the web of our unconscious human existence. All in this world appears to be so real; how can it be anything but Real? The eyes that see through duality only see duality. However, the eyes that see through unity, discern Truth from illusion. But this vision is not handed over simply for the asking. No, this is not how it works.

The gift of true vision is earned, not given, and with each conscious death of the personality, the soul's light takes root in the space thus created. Then, this body, this life, becomes a platform for the awakened soul to soar – to fulfill its goals and realize its intentions. Ultimately, such a presence becomes a bridge between heaven and earth, consciousness and unconsciousness, God and humanity. For the awakened soul is an embodiment of compassion and the heart that loves for love's sake.

In An Ecstatic State is an intimate journey of healing, awakening, and transformation. Take the time to read and digest. Let the words feed and nourish that part of you that remembers. More and more, you will find that the heart begins to speak a familiar tone that stirs the slumbering soul. This awakening allows for the recognition and resurgence of Self and the Universal Truths that reside within each conscious breath.

It is my wish and intention that every being be awakened to its full potential, realizing the soul's true capacity for greatness – and living into that greatness. May this poetry be an inspirational spark, igniting the path of remembrance.

Enjoy the journey!

Joseph Aldo
January 2015
Brooklyn, NY

IN THIS BOAT TOGETHER

We are all
in this boat together
you and I.

The journey is alone.

However,
alone we are together
in this boat of transfiguration
that shifts and changes as each one of us
goes through the tumult of emotions within bodies of water.
Waves of torrent sweep over us
purifying the darkness
revealing the Light.

Take a look around and you will see
that we are all one together
alone in the world
together
transforming
at the speed of thought.

The Light of Consciousness
intensifies the darkness of our ignorance
awakening us to the wisdom forever present within.

In this boat we are together
lover and Beloved
sharing a most
tender
kiss.

THE SUFFERING

The suffering
so intense
not a soul can relate.

If I thought
for one moment
that this was solely for me
surely, I would have ended this journey sooner.

But there is the awareness
that I am a leaf blowing in the spiritual wind
being guided and directed, tossed and turned for reasons so mysterious
that the understanding would return me to my source
and the game . . . the game would be over.

So I allow time and space to ravage me
until there is nothing left but bones tossed on the barren earth;
left for dead, it would appear, the journey ended.

But then, from the hairline crack on that lifeless, brittle bone
a drip of marrow would appear and jump into the earth so dry.
From this union, a garden so lush would emerge
and many, many will come to sit on the grass.

Then, each blade would speak
to the marrow in each bone of every being
sharing the road taken, soothing the suffering soul
a much needed balm to soothe the suffering.

Thus, my life is lived as an offering
to nourish those journeying
seeking the answers
to the mysterious
unsolvable

THIS GRIEF

This grief . . .
this grief that turns into a puddle
that turns into an ocean
returns to me daily.

I wonder . . .
when, when will this end?
Soon, soon, I hear.

For there is a well that is forming
taking me to a depth of soul that could not be achieved
without the journey of loss – without the journey of many losses.

The path to reclaiming the soul is one of suffering.

When the heart gazes into the mirror of man
it realizes it is bound by a life of lies
cherished so deeply
that it forms a thick shell
from which reality is perceived
life is engaged and relationships are regarded.
But there is no connection from this place
for there is no heart to touch
no vulnerability
to share.

This grief . . .
the catalyst that leads to the great awakening . . .
a drop in the well that echoes the chambers of the heart
stirring the suffering into an emotional catharsis
that forms a hatchet whose sole purpose
is to CRACK THAT SHELL
revealing the doorway
that ultimately leads
the soul of man
back into the
heart of
God.

I WANT TO FIT IN!

I WANT TO FIT IN!

Gap me!
Gucci me!
Fast food me!

Hurry me up in this gushing river of humanity!

Just let me be like the rest of them
running from moment to moment
holding my breath, void of spirit
or a conscience that beckons me to live.

I'm tired of being the salmon
continually swimming upstream
death after death after death.

Can't I just float for once
half-dead, somewhat alive in this sea of humanity
claiming I'm accomplishing something
because I'm busy?

Why? Why?
Why not me to be like the rest of them?

I want the bliss of ignorance, the cataracts of insight.
Blind me to the truth 'cause it ain't easy being awake!

Please! Please! Please!
Lull me to sleep with your advertisements
force-feeding me into this stream of consumerism
buying myself into a glorious state of catatonia.

Happy, happy,
happy they seem in their stupor of isms.
At least they belong to something
even if it is a delusion.

But I . . .

I belong to nothing

for the abyss is my home

and the void

my lover.

And I . . .

I cease to exist

more and more

each

day.

I am frightened

by the loss of my connection

to disconnection.

Who will I be

when the abyss takes me

when the emptiness consumes me?

I lay in the arms of the void, pondering my dissolution.

Once awake, I've been told, there is no sleep to hide behind.

And the madness that befriends me? . . .

The madness is simply a reflection

of the ecstasy

to come.

WHO AM I?

And God inquired:
"What is your question, my beloved?"
I responded: "Who am I?"

And God replied:
"You are the marriage between
the sun and the moon
the earth and the sky
the wind and the rain
the form and the formless.

"You are a limited concept born of the Infinite Mind
a contraction birthed from a wound.
You are a molecule asleep in a dream
the universe pregnant with potential.

"You are the manifestation
of your wildest dreams and worst nightmares
of your most exquisite of experiences and
the challenges you call to yourself.

"You are the designer of your destiny
that which arises from the choices you make.
Consciousness is the palette with which to create;
Unconsciousness is the hatchet with which to destroy.

"Either way, it is your choice, not Mine.

"Therefore, do not call upon Me with tears of blame
questioning why I have created such a world.

"I created you with the absolute freedom to choose.

"For the world is a manifestation
of your will and the agreement of all wills combined.
Every day you are free to choose heaven or hell
for each is a reality brought forth into existence
by your individual and collective visions.

"You are who you decide to be
in each moment
for you are the builder
of your own life
not I.

"I Am
the architect
and I have created
the most perfect blueprint
from which to live
a conscious
life.

"All you must do
is follow the laws of Nature
for She shall guide and nourish you
reminding you of those Truths Eternal
inherent within Her delicate balance
within Her perfected blossoms
within the tiniest of seeds
from which all of life
is sustained and
evolves.

"The masters
who walked in your world
were indeed cosmic emissaries –
great reflectors of light embodying The Infinite.

"You too are an incarnation of greatest proportion
for the divine spark resides within you too.
And you too shall achieve all that
the masters attained –
and greater
still.

"Cultivate
that divine spark
until it becomes an Eternal Flame
illuminating the Earth with the Light of Truth
that one day you may become
the heaven of your
dreams.

"So . . .
my beloved sweet soul . . .
asking the question: 'Who am I?'
will dissolve the false notions, ideas, and beliefs
of whom you are not, returning you to that pure state of Self
where your heart and My heart beat as one
where heaven on Earth is realized
through your every step
your every word
your every
breath."

IT'S ALL OVER!

Do you think
that I understand
what is happening to me?

Do you think
that I know
where all of this is going?

Do you think
for one moment
that I am in control?

Don't kid yourself.
When God comes knocking at the door
IT'S ALL OVER!

THAT'S WHAT INSANITY IS

I think I've figured it out.

God just wants to get into my bones
and go for a walk.

That's what insanity is!

What a relief.

I thought there was something wrong with me
that I was in need of some prescription
to restore me back to "normal."

But *normal*, I realize, is the kite flying the man.
What's up is down and what's down is up
in this contraption called "reality."

And the madness I endure . . .
the madness, is coming down to Earth
and letting God walk in my bones.

Let me tell you something:
It ain't easy letting God in
'cause He's got big feet
and likes to run –
FAST!

HOW MANY TIMES?

And God pleaded:

"My beloved,
how many times do you need for Me
to ring the bells of consciousness upside your head
before realizing that you and I
are inseparable?

"How many mantras
do you need for Me to utter
before you come banging on the door
demanding I open up
and let you in?

"How many prayers
in how many religions
do you need for Me to recite
before you are liberated from
your self-imposed maya
and awaken to the
Infinite Mind
I AM?

"And how many psalms
do you need for Me to serenade
before your ears transcend
the cacophony of chaos
you call intelligence
and merge into
the sweet
silence
I AM?

"My beloved,

how many tears must you shed

before you realize that your heart *is* My heart

that your suffering is the path and not the destination

that your free will is My gift to you

by which you

can come

home?

"I AM
the Alpha and the Omega
the Sound and the Silence
the Prayer and the Praying.

"I AM the Light –
and the Shadow it creates.

"My beloved,
as much as you enjoy the ride
and are mesmerized by the dazzling scenery
it is time to get off the boat of duality
and dive into My ocean
of

B
L
I
S
S
s
s
s
s

BREAK THE MIRROR

BREAK THE MIRROR INTO A MILLION PIECES!

Shatter the illusion by daring to face it –
EVERY LAST BIT.

Remind it of its essence
by introducing it to your heart.

Then . . . embrace it.

Then . . . love it.

Then . . . welcome it home.

A SHATTERING MESS

My existence
is a shattering mess.

This thing called "my life"
is melting before my lamenting eyes.

I don't much know what to call this life
that I had heretofore
confidently
emphatically
regarded "mine."

I'd been walking through
what appeared to be MY life
a reality I had chosen, or so I thought
only to realize that life had been living me.

I had not chosen it.

Rather,
a default program had been defined
proclaiming I am to live the life
set forth by my forefathers
delineated within DNA
from proclivities
to thoughts
to sex
and even
to my destiny.

At some point
one has to take a stand
and declare:

Enough!

I HAVE HAD ENOUGH!

. . . of living

someone else's life

of living someone else's lie.

I can no longer wade in the muck

imagining that I am sailing the open seas.

For I have been too long possessed

by the familial archetypes

formulating my

E V E R Y

M O V E

walking in my

E V E R Y

S T E P

I care not

what "they" think

for *they* who would stop me

walk among the living dead

surviving to maintain

the stagnation

so named

status

quo

NO

I care not

what they think

for it is my mission

to extract the essence of Me

from this configuration called family

to decidedly differentiate

this genius

from that genus

for it is time

to create

my own

myth

N

O

W

MAYA

She comes to me
as glorious as can be
the queen of illusion
Maya is all I see.

Pleasure is the name of the game
over and over again –
food, sex, sleep
food, sex, sleep
that is all I seek.

There must be an end to this black hole;
it keeps me a prisoner growing old.
I seek the answers from the world unseen;
there appears to be no end to this dream.

There has to be a finality
to this eternal joy ride I call insanity.

For I am trickling down
soul spiraling round and round;
Circling the already known world
I seek to unfurl;
Reaching for the Earth
my soul longs to give birth.

And I have felt that seed within
growing ever so slowly with clear intention
waiting for me to rain and sun upon its glory
I know that deep within is another story.

Thus far I've been starved at the king's table
body lusting for those things insatiable
taking all I can get
handfuls of the world
and yet . . .

The dissatisfaction remains
the boredom sustains.
But I know that I must fulfill
this human journey still
until I desire something more
than the trinkets Maya leaves at my door.

Perhaps the next time she advances
I will simply deny her hypnotic glances
for how can I continue this life
of no peace – only strife?

"If not Maya," she does inquire,
"what is it you desire?"
And to this I would not resist:
"It is only death I can envision
death to this world and its beautiful prison
in exchange for the opening of my eyes
with which I may realize
the wisdom of the Universe
and the Eternal Truths in verse."

And to this she does concede
a declaration certain with surrender:
"It is yours for the asking, my son.
Welcome home.
The journey is done."

BEYOND
SUPERFICIAL

To focus on the superficial is
to simply scratch the surface of the soul.

What is external is but a blurry picture of possibility
shrouded in the confusion of man's distortion of the Truth.

A doorway, if never opened, can never reveal what lies inside.

What use is it to hold onto a seed and never show it the light of day?

What is the purpose of a life if not to unearth the beliefs of the mind that fears
and journey into the world of infinite intelligence within the heart that loves?

That tree
for all its beauty and blossoms
finds its strength in its roots.
Beauty is only as beautiful
as the roots are reaching
for what's a soul worth
if not its capacity to
extend its light
deeply into
humanity?

FIND YOUR PASSION

A watered-down version of God
JUST WON'T DO!

Find your passion
AND
LIVE IT
so completely
as if your life depends upon it
as if the whole of existence depends upon it

BECAUSE
IT
DOES!

THIS COSMIC GIFT

This cosmic gift
is not some precious jewel
to be set aside and safely locked away
for some future time in existence.

It wants to shine NOW!

It wants to be revealed
THROUGH YOU
for all its potency
for all its authenticity
and the Truth it inspires.

It is up to you
To CONTAIN that which cannot be contained
To GROUND that which cannot be grounded
To EMBODY A PARADOX whose very expression
destroys the foundation upon which it exists.

You are the one
who has chosen the impossible
but not the improbable.

Through you
a force moves that cannot be understood
and will not be understood by the mechanism of mind.

The fruit of the tree of knowledge is not yours to eat
for you cannot embody The Mystery. However,
The Mystery can embody you.

Surrender
to the stream of consciousness
that flows through you
for IT IS YOU
the you beyond the body
beyond the mind
beyond space
and time.

Let yourself be consumed
absorbed back into the Truth
that you may serve as a beacon
awakening the slumbering souls
returning them home
home to the Light.

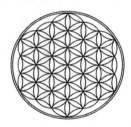

I DANCE 'CAUSE
THIS IS MY CHURCH!

I dance 'cause
this is my church!

When the music starts
God appears, grabs my hand
and we work that floor like nobody's business.

Of course,
I can't keep up with the Supreme One
as He spins me round and round
illusions flying left and right
as they scurry away
away from the
Light.

I laugh hysterically
as God dips me yet one more time.
My spectacles go flying and the drink I am nursing
shatters to the ground – red wine blesses
the parquet floor.

"Keep up!" He says,
"For the night is young and My love for you is endless.
I won't stop 'til you are thoroughly cooked
and perfectly soul-seasoned!

"By the time this night is over
you're not gonna know what hit ya.
Past and future shall collide and through you
a new world shall be born.

"Finally,
you will know what it is to be free
to no longer be ruled by the delusions mass produced.
For you shall be a clear ray
of My divine Light.

"Just remember
to turn up the music night after night
'cause I've always got new moves for you
that are gonna spin your paradigm on its head
creating a vortex and a path
that leads from here
to Eternity!"

EVER ETERNAL SOUL

I don't know
if one would call
what I am experiencing
an agitation
an inspiration
a realization
or simply
death
the ending
to an old story
carrying the burdens
of the mothers and fathers
possessions somehow imposed
adopted and absorbed through proximity
where a miasmatic mess realizes its completion
in this moment of madness that is essentially mine
as I drop down into the depths of surrender
a choice that I make for freedom
regardless of the fears
the unknown fears
wishing to claim
existence
as its
own

but
there's
not much
in this world
that prepares one
for such an experience
as identity is a slippery slope
defined by external circumstances
and a collection of familial experiences
rather than a personal journey of discovery
whereby one deconstructs and dissolves
dropping layer upon layer upon layer
the unessential qualities of Self
fine tuning and polishing
that sacred being
Ever Eternal
Soul

JUMP!

One night
God woke me up, screaming:
"I gave you a universe
and you are trying to put it into a star!
What's up with that?!

"You are so much more than
what you believe
what you perceive
what you have learned.

"Go beyond the dream and step into The Vision.
YOU CAN FULFILL THE VISION.

"Rather than getting lost in the letter of the law
REALIZE THE ESSENCE OF THE TEACHINGS.
Then, become an EMBODIMENT
of *that* Essence.

"YOU ARE THE PIONEER
leading the way through uncharted territories.
Therefore, you must go beyond what is written
beyond what is known.

"YOU ARE THE KEEPER
of that which has yet to be discovered
but shall be uncovered through you.

"So when you make it to the point of no return
where mind and heart converge
step to the edge of the cliff
take a deep . . . deep
breath and . . .

J
U
M
P
!

"Jump as far and as high as you can
knowing that you are charting new territory.

"There is no way to realize a new discovery
but to let go of whom you have been.
Knowledge serves one purpose:
To get you from here
to there.

"However,
once you arrive
you must release the teachings
and embody The Teacher."

THERE IS NOTHING WRONG

There is nothing wrong
with the body, its desires and form.
It is a sacred vessel made from Love
created that you may journey
through the dream of separation
awakening to the illusion of identification
remembering your soul's song
as you return to that place
of oneness.

Surrender
into the body
with which you have
been blessed.

Lose yourself
in the beauty of the senses
in the subtlety of the feelings
in the intensity of the emotions
celebrating the bliss of union
with all that you come
in contact.

Relax
into the body
releasing all judgments
abandoning all beliefs of separation
for the body is the beginning and the end
of a journey that goes round and round
and until it becomes fully embraced
the body is the source of suffering
rather than The Source Itself.

SO
UNHESITATINGLY
UNHINDERED

Give over to me

that vulnerability

that passion

that heart

that I may experience

a kiss

so unhesitatingly unhindered

and totally committed to transforming you and I

into a messy pool of God only knows what

that we may become something greater

than you or I could ever be

individually

for this union

negates the notion

insisting man and God

are separate bedfellows

reigniting the fire of truth

that passion unbridled can

catalyze and catapult

the soul of man

into the heart

of God

THAT KISS

That kiss . . .
you planted in my garden.

That kiss . . .
you left at my doorstep.

THAT KISS!
You should have warned me! . . .
that my life would never EVER be the same
that my existence would go ablaze
that I would come to realize
all I reasoned was true
was but a shadow
of the Truth.

That kiss
remains with me still
moving through every cell
SETTING ME ON FIRE.

The passion I cannot contain!
It consumes me – not the *real* me
but the lies I've devised and called my Self
they burn, and I welcome it.

For this vortex of Love
is EVERYTHING.

I care not
about anything else
for there is no relevance
without *this* Love.

I shall hold onto that kiss
for no verse in any spiritual opus
has ever moved me
in this way . . .
in my body.

Actually
as I recall
the emphasis
has been abstention
from all earthly passions
that lust has no place in Love
that the body of man or woman
is not welcome in the heart of God.

But I will tell you this: IT IS NOT TRUE!
For God is longing to get into these bodies.

HE wants to make Love
to me
to you
through US.

He wants to taste our mouths
ripe with desire, as tongues engage.

He wants to feel our flesh
warm and aroused, as we embrace.

He wants to smell the sweet scent of Love
as pores exude the fires of passion
gazing into those beautiful eyes
as they surrender . . .
past and future melting
so vulnerably into the moment.

He wants to hold those tender hearts
in His hands
as . . . we . . . climax . . .

In Truth
we are His creation
designed in His likeness.
Why then deny the impulses?
For they are God's calling
calling us back to Him
through the senses
rather than
in spite of them.

I give up
rationalizing away
the body's myriad urges.

Instead
I shall descend
deeper into this earthly domain
letting God in on all my desires
making an altar of this body
and seeing as sacred
that which has
formerly been
erroneously
considered
profane.

That kiss . . .
a gift of presence
you bestowed upon me
that I may remember
what it means
to make Love
and
to be Love.

IF YOU LET ME IN

One morning
God shared His longing with me . . .

"If you let Me in
I could see through your eyes
and breathe through your body.
I would feel through your senses
and laugh through your heart.
I would love everything, no matter what
for all would be a part of Me
seen unseen, living beyond the dream.

"I would be in a continual state of ecstasy
just to be a part of your reality
living life so fully . . .
laughing – crying
loving – longing
dancing – falling . . .
I would be so happy to be welcomed
into the world created
as it creates.

"And you . . .
you would know Me as I
reflected through your mind
navigated through your body
shared through your heart.

"You would awaken to a world so mysterious
known only to those who choose Me –
seeing beyond sight, knowing beyond knowledge
loving beyond the limitations of expectancy.

"You
would soar
above and beyond
delusions senselessly designed
by the narrow perceptions
propelled by a mind
driven by fear
judgment
separation
guilt and sorrow.
You would come to know
that all and everything exists
for Me, as Me, through Me, and nothing
ABSOLUTELY NOTHING
is wrong . . .
or right.

"Call Me to you
as I call you to Me
that we may be lover and Beloved
finally merged into one body
seeing through the one eye
thinking with one mind
loving through the
one heart."

BECOME LOVE ITSELF

Tonight I cried: "It's too much!
Stop loving me so much
'cause I can't take it!"

And God said:
"But I want you back, with Me
in My arms, loving Me."

"Yes, yes!" I said,
"I know what you want.
But your Love is so intense
I don't know how to contain it."

And God lovingly responded:
"Become like the colander, full of holes
so that the Love I pour into you
reaches everyone.

"Then,
you shall be a living waterfall
of My Infinite Grace.

"Purge yourself of life's many injustices.
Forgive and forget what wrongs
have been done.

"Once you are empty
drink from Love's merciful stream
filling yourself fully with compassion
that one day you may become
Love Itself."

SHHHHHHH . . .

Shhhhhhh . . .
I have something to say to you.
Yes, I do have something to say to you.

Now I don't know how you are going to take this
as you are so full of the past
and I don't know how much room
you have for the present.

Nonetheless,
I am going to say it
right here, right now, to you
the one before me.

I know you may not believe me
as you are so convinced of the contrary
and have proof, journals of proof
of the many crimes against
your heart.

However,
you must believe me when I say this
for IT IS TRUE.

And I am going against the grain sharing this bit with you.

F'ordinarily, I would think about this for so long
that this blossom rarely bloomed
would quickly lose its
fragrance.

But today
I am here RIGHT NOW.
And tomorrow? Tomorrow I don't know
who or what or where
I shall be.

But I am here

NOW

and this . . .

THIS is all that matters.

So . . .

close your eyes . . .

take a deep, deep breath . . .

open your heart . . .

and receive this:

I LOVE YOU.

ONE DAY LOVE BARGED IN

One day
Love barged in, screaming:
"What the heaven are you doing?!"

I swung my head around, shocked
dismayed at Love's aggression:
"What? What's wrong?"

"I told you," She cried, "Let go! LET IT ALL GO!
The anger, the fear, the hatred –
useless, all useless!"

I bowed my head in shame for I knew I was to blame
for Her uproarious upset and crazed chastisements.

She continued . . .
"There's one game, one game only in this world of form.

"What's the point of a life so free
if not to use your heart for the purpose it was conceived?

"Who are you creature of judgment
the one who has forgotten that to judge others
is to judge one's self?

"If you want to win this game, then surrender everything
EVERYTHING that is not Love.

"For what's a life worth
if not to actualize the heart's objective:
To know itself by loving others unconditionally."

She sighed . . .
"My infinite patience is wearing thin . . .

"How many tests must I send you
before you awaken to your heart's longing
for Love?

"Suffering is not
an external
device.

"To suffer
is to ignore
is to ignorate –
to generate something
other than Love.

"Snap out of it!
STOP THIS MADNESS!
Forgive – FORGIVE
and come home
to Me.

"Release.
Surrender.
Compassionize.
Unificate.
Love.

N
O
W
!
"

TO LET LOVE IN

To let Love in
is no thoughtless task
for what we call an open heart
is often a mind in the shape of a fist
holding a list of conditions
that need to be fulfilled
if you and I are to share
a true moment
of intimacy.

To let Love in
the heart of one must see
through the heart of the other
dissolving those isolating thoughts of "me" or "you"
resisting the demands of "I want" or "I need"
releasing the compulsion to take
surrendering the impulse
to be gratified
choosing instead
to give unconditionally
from this place of
vulnerability
openness
humility.

To let Love in
we must die to our defenses
unlearning the mechanisms of manipulation
for the heart cannot – and will not – be compromised.
It's either ALL or nothing when it comes to Love
for the heart does not discriminate.
Love flows freely, otherwise
it is not Love.

To let Love in
we must let Love out.
Break the dam that claims
Love should be rationed
that the heart must be cautious
that one must be worthy
to receive the gift
of Love.

ALL are worthy
to receive Love
ALL-WAYS.

To let Love in
release the past
surrender the mind
descend into the heart
listen to the voice of your soul
respond with kindness
hold and be held
with exquisite
presence.

To let Love in
love indiscriminately
that your heart may be
the bridge to compassion
for to give is to receive
to receive is to give.
When Love flows
the essence
of a soul
is released.
That perfume
is the realization
of a life fulfilled.

I WILL BE THERE STILL

I wish to lie with you
and hold you close to my heart.

I feel your resistance
the struggle to free yourself from my embrace.
But I won't let go – EVER.

I will hold you
until the anger turns to grief
and the tendency to strike softens to tears that soak us both
until we are dripping, dripping with the sadness and pain
of all that occurred over and over again
to harden your tender heart.

And when those tears overflow
creating a river so full
I will be there still
as the banks
holding you ever so closely
never to let you go.

And when the river can be contained no more
surging into the oceans so vast
I will be there still
as the beaches and the basins
caressing your every wave
letting you ebb and flow
inhale and exhale
in my arms
outstretched.

And when the oceans expand
to take over the land
I will be there still
as the salt of the Earth
holding every tear you've ever shed
keeping them close to my heart
loving you forever
and ever
still.

FOR LOVE'S SAKE

One day I asked God:
"So what's the purpose of this life?"

And He responded:
"To be loving wherever you go."

And I countered:
"But where do I start?"

"Start with yourself," He said.

"But how do I begin this journey
for there is much ground to cover
so much unforgiveness to release?"

"Begin with that which lies on the surface.
Then, work your way inwards until you find your heart.

"Once you reach it, lovingly break it
so that you no longer worry about your own needs.
Destroy it, so that your love of self no longer stands in the way
of your love for others.

"When this is achieved
you will have realized the purpose of life
and the goal of being loving will be fulfilled
in you, through you, as you.

"For you will be an embodiment
of the heart that loves
for Love's sake."

A LOVE SO GREAT

What will it take
to experience a love so great?

What will it take
to allow your heart to feel deeply
that the rivers would threaten to swell
beyond the banks so contained
and tears would overflow
unrestrained?

What will it take
to be free from all the stories –
the pain, the sadness, the loneliness –
to clear the mind of the many rationalizations
of how, when, and where to have
those experiences of
the heart?

What will it take
for you to love freely – always?

Who would you be
if Love possessed you
like the rest of your life possesses you?

Who would you be
if your bank account was your Love account
if abundance was measured by the fullness of your heart
and how much you shared
rather than acquired?

Who would you be
if
like a child
you were allowed
to live each moment
fully feel each experience
relax into every cathartic emotion
without a mind
always ready
to turn
water
into
ice?

Who would you be
if Life took you by the hand like a loving parent
brought you to an open field
and said:

"RUN!
Run as fast as you can

and when you feel like it
Rest

and when you feel like it
Eat

and when you feel like it
Dream."

Who would you be
if you were this free
but a love so great.

THE MEMORY OF LOVE
Dedicated to Samyama

The child arises within her
eyes wide open
seeing the unseen
marveling at God's divine creation.

Beauty is painted
within the irises of her gaze
for that is all she sees
as she pierces the veil of illusion
the cocoon of maya
surrounding the forgetful soul.

Her love burrows deep
deep within the fortress of fear
melting the metal swords
that protect the sweet and tender heart.

"Give it to me!" she cries,
"For I will hold your heart close
so close to my own
tender heart.

"And soon . . .
soon your heart too shall beat as mine.
And the memory of Love
I share with you
my beloved."

THE GODDESS
for Candace

She stands there
heart in hands for all to see.
Venus sits in the orbits of her eyes;
the well of love goes deep
very, very deep.

The Mother that is Earth
recognizes her daughter – a goddess in form
extending from her roots
arising from the ocean's depths.
She comes to life
as life itself.

Unfurling as the fern . . .
she begins to move
. . . slowly
as she listens
sensing the rhythm
of her Mother's heartbeat.

All of Nature bows before her
as the elements cease their preoccupations
gazing in awe at the moonlit form
radiant before them.

Her Mother's heartbeat quickens
and the goddess responds by drumming her feet.
Her voice trembles, vibrating with lyrical anticipation
as her body quakes, erupting in rhythmic dance
moving to the music within her heart while
summoning the song within her soul.

The darkness waits
expectantly...

Spinning
round and round
she unravels her ecstasy.

Her whole being bellows –
a rapturous howl only the night
could contain.

A trance-like intoxication saturates her soul
as she flows to Mother Earth's universal hymn:
"Love one another and all that is," She proclaims,
"for you and I, and all that is, exist
as lover and Beloved."

The elements
unable to bridle their bliss
explode in their embrace of the goddess
lifting her in a whirlwind of passion.
A celebration of the Earth is she.

"We are at your command," they announce,
"and with every intention you intone
know that it is deemed so."

The dance slows to a still
as the elements merge with her form.
A quiet smile shines in satisfaction
sensing the flow of all that is
within, around and through her.

Upon her Mother's bosom she lies
as Grandmother Moon summons dreamtime.
"Sleep, my child," she whispers, "and remember to weave
in the darkest of dark, the tapestry of Love
that all may find solace
in your presence –
the goddess."

THE LOTUS
for Sequoia

She expands before me
reaching . . .
reaching . . . . . .
reaching beyond the muck of the Earth
realizing in each unfolding petal
the brilliance of her heart
the ecstasy of her soul
and the glory of her connection
to the Mother below, the Father above.

With an awareness so pure, a scent so sublime
she shares her essence with everyone
befriending with her beauty
expressions of unity –
a life so fully lived
a love so fully embraced.

For she is an embodiment of the heart that endures
allowing sorrow and grief to pass gracefully through her
destroying her, over and over and over again
dropping one petal . . . then another . . .
then another still . . .
until she is
no more.

Invisible to the waking world
she descends
deep
deep into dormancy
awaiting . . . awaiting . . .

Silently she weeps
quietly cultivating her internal fire
burning away the heartache of the past
as she visions through the flames
the future unfolding . . .

The passion builds
as the lotus roots . . .
deeper . . .
deeper . . . . . .
deeper into the Mother, piercing Her heart
gathering the ever-flowing
nurturing nectar
of Love.

Once full,
she weeps again, wailing in ecstasy
as the vision arises within her:
"I AM HERE!
THE TIME IS NOW!"

The next breath cracks her whole being
breaking her beyond her known identity
compelling her to expand . . .
Expand . . .
EXPAND . . . .

The waiting is over.

Patience and perseverance
have transmuted in the fires of transformation.
Purity and virtuosity have ascended.
The alchemical gold is achieved.

The internal fires blaze with expectancy
as the lotus reaches from the depths
of the cool waters . . .

SHE CAN BE CONTAINED NO MORE

With grace and poise
she humbly reenters the world
caressing the water's edge
creating but a slight . . .
subtle . . .
ripple . . . . . .
as she reveals her beauty
. . . reaching
. . . . . . reaching
reaching from the depths of her Mother
to the heights of her Father
one
expanding
petal
at
a
time . . .

THE TRUE SEEKER LOOKS WITHIN

The true seeker looks within
that he may end his external search
for the Beloved.

Outside are the pitfalls that lead him back
back to his Self.

He neither avoids nor turns away from the wounds.

Instead, he takes the journey so circuitous
that it spins him round, upside down, inside out
forcing him to face the illusions head on
reclaiming the power to create
transforming the materials of maya
using them to fashion a new life
as the ruler of worlds –
all worlds.

Only he who confronts the darkness
facing his fears boldly
shall be the master of masters
and king of kings.

Once this is achieved
and there is no more to brave
death will come knocking on his door
a door of transparency
and he shall embrace death
as he embraces new life.

Then lover and Beloved
shall once again
unite.

DEATH THE BELOVED

Ravaged by the Light I am
swirling in a whirlwind of transformation.

Slowly, I am consumed of what I know, of who I claim to be.

Left to die, I lie outstretched on the cross of my burdens.

My mind pecks at the rotting flesh of my non-existence commanding me to move
to resume the unconscious dance of the non-living.

"What do you know of death," it screams, "to hand it over your life?!
A fool's journey you have undertaken.
A messianic moron you have become."

A martyr I may be, but the path I've not chosen
for *it* has chosen me.

Resist as I may, it persists this calling.

But I fight it no more
neither you, my ignorant mind
nor the Light that blinds me night after night.

The path of least resistance I give of myself.
And death . . . it summons no more
for we are now lovers – inseparable.

Each time it reaches for my hand
I surrender my whole body
because through death
I attain true life.

THE FIRE OF LONGING

Sit
in the fire of longing.
Be with the bewilderment.
Commit to the chaos of confusion
while you journey in search of the Self
disoriented as to your true identity
wishing for that moment when
the awakened Self can be
fully Realized.

Day after day after day
let the weariness from longing consume you
until you have completely burned
scorched by the timbers
of desire.

Do not act.
Do not move.
Do not distract.

Stay with the longing.

Life is a journey of transformation.
All that arises are but fleeting memories of former selves
possessions deluded as to their true identities.
Let the ghosts of those memories ascend
until all that remains is the Self.

The temptations to engage
dances with the dead
will be fierce.

However,
the key to liberation is
TO OBSERVE –
observe as the past plays itself out.

Floods of emotion will surge
cascading throughout every wound
searching to attach to a painful memory
and find expression, once again
in the realm of illusion.

Watch in
and watch out
discerning past from present.
Do not run away from, nor engage in
the mania that emerges.

Instead,
integrate these uprisings
for they are the raw materials
utilized in the cauldron of transformation
necessary for the alchemical shift
that awaits you.

Sit
in the fire of longing.

Transmute the "negativity" that burdens you.

This is the ancient formula that transforms darkness into Light.

Realize, the greater the shadow, the greater the potential for illumination.

This journey can be intense, arduous, and disheartening.

But if life was without its challenges
you would not know the power within fire
and how the passion from longing
leads the caterpillar to turn
more and more
inward...

until something happens . . .
until something spectacular happens . . .
where the Self, always known
finally becomes
Realized.

IN LOVE'S SWEET EMBRACE

Death
a welcome doorway
revealing both past and future
in one conscious breath.

In the presence of death
all worlds collide and chaos reigns.
Dark clouds pour forth the cleansing waters
overcoming the shadows of existence.

Death, indeed, is a welcome doorway
where fear and Love battle it out –
one fighting, the other forgiving.

Who do you think will win?

Try to resist
the sweetness in a lover's gaze
the thoughtfulness from words of praise
the loving touch of a warm embrace.

You want to flee from the feelings that arise
when intimacy touches the wounds
for they are so real
the pain, the anger, the grief.
But they are the distortions of Love
possessions whose destiny is the altar of sacrifice.

All will burn and transmute back into their original form: Love.

So when Love comes knocking on your door
do not put up your armor of defenses
with a hardened heart.

Instead
soften . . . melt . . .
as you step through the doorway of death
for life awaits you on the other side
in Love's sweet embrace.

WHO WOULD WE BE WERE WE WED?

One morning
God woke me up, weeping:

"Today,
you are the lover and I . . .
I am the Beloved.

"Tomorrow,
I am the Lover and you . . .
you are the beloved.

"We are forever nearing one another
yet we remain always separate
in our longing.

"Who would we be
if lover and Beloved merged
where the heart's beating
was both the call and response
continuously echoing the one sound
within the one body?

"Who would we be were we wed
no longer nearing but finally one?"

WILL YOU DROP THE BUCKET?

You may be afraid to acknowledge
the depths of this love.

But I know how deep
the well goes.

The question is:
Will you

d

r

o

p

the
bucket?

LOVE

One day
while walking through the park with God
She had this to say:

"Love is the doorway to freedom
from all limitation
all delusions of duality
all suffering.

"Love is the one place on Earth where the game is won
where there are no questions to be answered
no doubts to overcome
for there is no mind to manage.

"I want you to know
Love is the destination – your destiny.
Everything else is a mere distraction
an obstacle on the road to Love.

"Whatever you do, do it for Love.
Seek It out, that you may know It
that you may be It
inside out.

"Love is like a river
always flowing, ever present.

JUMP IN!

"It doesn't matter if you are afraid.
It doesn't matter if you know how to swim.
It doesn't even matter if the river takes you
and breaks you over the rocks.

"All that matters is that you go for it
that you dive in and learn the ways of Love
for there is no toe dipping when it comes to *this* river.
It's either all or nothing!

"And how can you succeed at Love without Love's failure?
How can you know Love – *truly* KNOW Love
without experiencing Its absence?

"There are no mistakes or failures on this journey
for each step of the way there is wisdom collected.
And when enough wisdom is gained
a vessel is formed to contain.
That vessel is YOU.

"Realize this:
The mind is clueless when it comes to Love.
Everything is good/bad, right/wrong, yours/mine.
There is no space for Love in such a paradigm.

"Not until the mind

drops

into

the heart

does it truly understand
anything.

"It is said that the human heart must break in order for Love to flow.
But the reality is, the mind has a stranglehold on the heart's freedom;
it is the dam that decides when, who and how much to love.

"However,
Love knows no limits, for It does not ration the infinite.

"Love gives of Itself spontaneously, without prompting, without restraint
unconcerned about Its wants or needs, or what It may lose or gain
in the intimate sharing that arises.

"Love never looks back or concerns Itself with the future
for Its only consideration is the moment
where lover and Beloved
dissolve into one.

"So you see,
in order for Love to truly be the guiding force in one's life
the mind must break open and release everything
yes
EVERYTHING.

"For what is considered wisdom to the mind
is madness to the heart.

"True knowledge arises
when the mind chooses to release
its limited perceptions and projections
into the silence of the heart.

"When the mind surrenders its opinions
desisting to defend its position in the world
its opposition will also
cease to exist.

"Finally,
the war of duality
shall transform into peace
and a drop of stillness shall descend
into the emptiness thus created.

"Then the marriage
between mind and heart
shall be realized.

"And Love . . .
Love will be free
to Love."

WHEN LOOKING THROUGH
THE EYES OF LOVE

When looking through the eyes of Love
there is no fear, only faith
no doubt, only trust
no surface, only soul
for there is no mind, only heart.

There is no other
for all encountered are the Beloved.

When looking through the eyes of Love
there's an open heart holding another's heart
with a tenderness so precious
that butterfly's wings could safely be held
and free to fly with equal grace.

When looking through the eyes of Love
the eyes that see through duality cease to exist
for time and space have no relevance
where Love is present.

When looking through the eyes of Love
I melt from the separate me
into the unified we
dissolving . . .
dissolving . . . . . .
past and future into this moment
where our united presence
births a being
greater than you or I
could ever be individually.

Thank you for seeing me for who I am
allowing me to see you for who you truly are
and for granting God the space
to reside within
this union.

TO WALK THIS PATH OF LOVE

Sleep is screaming me to bed.

But I delay . . .

to write one more verse . . .

to paint one more picture . . .

of the love I feel for you.

Our meeting has turned you upside down
and me inside out.

Finally,
we are set straight
to walk this path of Love.

THE LOVER

Enveloped by His body
I am consumed.

An embrace so complete
I both lose and find myself
in the same breath.

A RELIGIOUS MAN

They ask me,
"Are you a religious man?"

And to that I say,
"Yes, a religious man I am.

"However,
I would also add that
although I am a religious man
I have no need for religion.

"For God and I
are close, intimate friends
and we have no need of a middleman
to translate His kiss
upon my brow."

GOD'S WILD CARD

I Am God's wild card.

He plays me
whenever He wants
to shake
things
up.

Just when you least expect it
you may find me in places
of a seemingly most inappropriate nature
doing what appears to be seemingly
most inappropriate things.

However,
behind every action is the divine hand
strumming the strings of my heart
bringing forth a sweet harmonic
that penetrates the barriers to Love
fully dissolving those tendencies to suffer
in a world where the extremes of right and wrong
create a chasm that confuses the sensitive soul
who simply wants to remember
what it is to live
in the heart
of God.

I Am God's wildcard.

He plays me
whenever He wants

to shake

things

∪ ⊓

•

I REMEMBER

I AM
unlike anyone
who has walked before
or who shall ever walk again.

I AM one who creates existence
by living and envisioning
in each moment
The Truth
tearing down
the illusions within
transforming the maya without.

There's no other way to effect change
except to consider one's Self the universe
rearranging the stars, the planets, the galaxies
until harmony is once again restored.

Then all universes will entrain.
Lower shall rise, base will alchemize
and the gold . . . the gold will be realized.

I remember how one conscious drop
in the slumbering sea of humanity
can awaken and transform
the whole of humanity.

That drop
I AM